ANNE GEDDES

Down in the Garden

Journal

ANNE GEDDES ™

ISBN 0-7683-2017-8

© Anne Geddes 1997

Published in 1998 by Photogenique Publishers (a division of Hodder Moa Beckett)
Studio 3.16, Axis Building, 1 Cleveland Road, Parnell
Auckland, New Zealand

USA edition published in 1998 by Cedco Publishing Company,
100 Pelican Way, San Rafael, CA 94901

Designed by Jane Seabrook
Produced by Kel Geddes
Color separations by Image Centre

Printed through South China Printing Co. Ltd., Hong Kong

Please write to us for a FREE FULL COLOR catalog of our fine Anne Geddes
calendars and books, Cedco Publishing Company, 100 Pelican Way,
San Rafael, CA 94901.
or, visit our website : www.cedco.com
10 9 8 7 6 5 4

Welcome to the world of Anne Geddes.

The images used in this journal are taken from Anne's latest collective work entitled *Down In The Garden*.

Anne says in her foreword to that book:
"I hope that, through my work as a photographer, I have been able to pass on my appreciation of the beauty and charm of little children. As adults we all need to stop occasionally and look at ourselves and our circumstances with an open mind and a sense of humor, and remember to appreciate the simple things in life, which are often the most important."

We hope that when using this journal you can record some of the simple, yet magic, moments of your life's journey.

Canterbury Belles